W9-CFW-961

Make
Your Own
Make It Go!

Make a

Pop Rocket

by Maddie Spalding

NORWOOD HOUSE PRESS

Norwood House Press
P.O. Box 316598
Chicago, Illinois 60631

For information regarding Norwood House Press, please visit our website at:
www.norwoodhousepress.com or call 866-565-2900.

LIBRARY OF CONGRESS CATALOGING-IN-PUBLICATION DATA

Names: Spalding, Maddie, 1990- author.
Title: Make a pop rocket / by Maddie Spalding.
Description: Chicago, Illinois : Norwood House Press, [2018] | Series: Make your own: make it go! | Includes bibliographical references and index.
Identifiers: LCCN 2018003225 (print) | LCCN 2018004754 (ebook) | ISBN 9781684041954 (ebook) | ISBN 9781599539232 (hardcover : alk. paper)
Subjects: LCSH: Rockets (Aeronautics)--Juvenile literature. | Handicraft--Juvenile literature.
Classification: LCC TL547 (ebook) | LCC TL547 .S71184 2018 (print) | DDC 745.592--dc23
LC record available at https://lccn.loc.gov/2018003225

312N—072018
Manufactured in the United States of America in North Mankato, Minnesota.

Contents

CHAPTER 1

All about Rockets

Rockets come in many shapes and sizes. The first rockets were built thousands of years ago. They were weapons. In the 1200s CE, Chinese soldiers filled bamboo tubes with gunpowder. Then they lit the gunpowder. Smoke and other gases formed inside the tube. These gases pushed the rocket into the air.

In the 1950s, rockets were created for space exploration. In 1957, a rocket sent the first **satellite** into space. Oil and liquid oxygen were mixed inside the rocket's engine. They were burned for fuel. Gases passed through the engine's nozzle at high speeds. This shot the rocket and satellite into space. Using common household items, you can make a pop rocket that will help you understand how full-size rockets work.

Pop rockets are models of full-size rockets. They are simple to make. The rocket is simply a small plastic canister. But it needs fuel to move. Pop rockets are powered by liquid fuel. Two common substances can be mixed for fuel in a pop rocket. Those are water

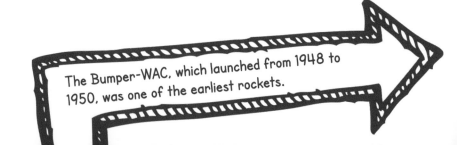

The Bumper-WAC, which launched from 1948 to 1950, was one of the earliest rockets.

Real rockets are launched by powerful explosions.

and Alka-Seltzer. Alka-Seltzer is a type of antacid tablet. These are used to treat upset stomachs.

Both water and Alka-Seltzer have **atoms**. Atoms are the basic pieces of matter that things are made of. Atoms come together in groups called **molecules**. A **chemical reaction** happens when two or more kinds of molecules interact.

During this chemical reaction, a **base** and an **acid** will be mixed. Alka-Seltzer tablets contain citric acid. They also contain baking soda. The base is the baking soda. Citric acid is the acid. The citric acid and baking soda are separate in the tablet. They do not interact with each other. When the tablet is dropped into water, the water dissolves it. The base and the acid then mix. This creates **carbon dioxide** gas. The gas fizzes in the water.

In a pop rocket, this reaction takes place in a plastic canister. The gas molecules inside the canister move fast. The molecules run into one another. This causes the carbon dioxide gas to expand. The gas pushes up against the lid of the canister. The lid acts as the rocket's nozzle. **Pressure** builds up. The gas pushes off the lid and pops it in the air.

All rockets are launched by **thrust**. Thrust is a force created by **accelerating** gas. Carbon dioxide acts as a thrust force. It pushes the canister up into the air. Thrust force moves a rocket because of the **Third Law of Motion**. This law says that every action has an equal and opposite reaction. The gas is pushed downward out of the nozzle. The thrust pushes up on the rocket. This makes the rocket shoot up into the air.

Parts of a Rocket

Fuel

Nose

Nozzle

Blast

Rockets need to be strong so they don't fall apart when they are up in the air.

CHAPTER 2

Making a Pop Rocket

Rockets need to be made from strong materials. But they also need to be light. The less the rockets weigh, the higher they can shoot up in the sky. Full-size rockets are often made from aluminum or other metals. Pop rockets are propelled by liquid fuel. Water is a liquid. But many materials **absorb** water. When water is absorbed, there is less water available for the chemical reaction. Plastic absorbs less water than wood. Plastic is also strong and lightweight.

The amount of fuel a rocket needs depends on its weight. Every object has weight. Weight is the force of **gravity** on an object. A rocket is launched when the thrust force is greater than the weight force. The thrust force acts opposite the weight force. It pushes the rocket up. Pop rockets are lightweight, so the thrust force needed to launch them is small. Large rockets weigh more. A greater thrust force is needed to launch them. For this reason, full-size rockets need large engines. The engine is filled with enough fuel to keep the rocket in the air for long periods of time.

A rocket has many nozzles to help launch it.

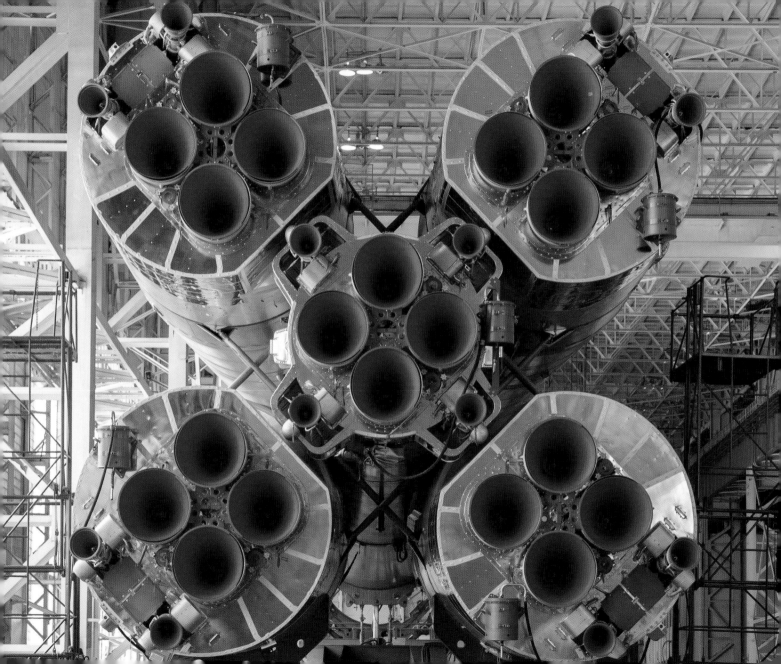

The height of the pop rocket's launch depends on the amount of substances used for the fuel. Just a small amount of water is needed. If too much water is used, there will be water left over after the chemical reaction. This will weigh down the rocket. Then it will not be able to go very high. Also, only a small amount of Alka-Seltzer is needed to create a chemical reaction.

The substances that are chosen for the pop rocket fuel affect how fast it will launch. Water temperature also affects reaction time. Molecules move faster in warm water than in cold water. The chemical reaction happens more quickly when molecules move faster. You will want the reaction to happen fast. But if the reaction

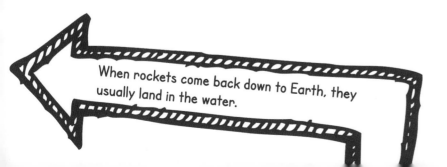
When rockets come back down to Earth, they usually land in the water.

happens too fast, you will not have time to set up your rocket. The rocket that you will make will need medium-warm water. Also, you should make sure that the lid on the canister can be shut tight. If the lid isn't tight, gas will escape. This will reduce the amount of thrust force.

If possible, do your pop rocket experiment outside. This way, you will have less mess to clean up. This experiment should also be done with adult help. Once you mix the water and the Alka-Seltzer inside the canister, sit back and watch the reaction happen. Within five to ten seconds, your rocket will pop up high into the air!

Materials Checklist

✓ 1 Alka-Seltzer tablet

✓ Water

✓ 1 small plastic canister with a tight snap-on lid

✓ Eye goggles (for protection)

✓ Plastic cup (optional)

Don't crush the tablet too small. You want to still have some of the tablet in chunks.

CHAPTER 3

Make It Go!

Now that you know how pop rockets work, let's put our knowledge to use and build one!

1. Fill the plastic canister two-thirds full with lukewarm water. Make sure the lid is completely separate from the canister.

2. Gently crush up one Alka-Seltzer tablet inside the packet. You can put the crushed tablet into the plastic cup if you like. Pouring from the cup can be easier than pouring directly from the packet.

3. Put on your eye goggles for protection.

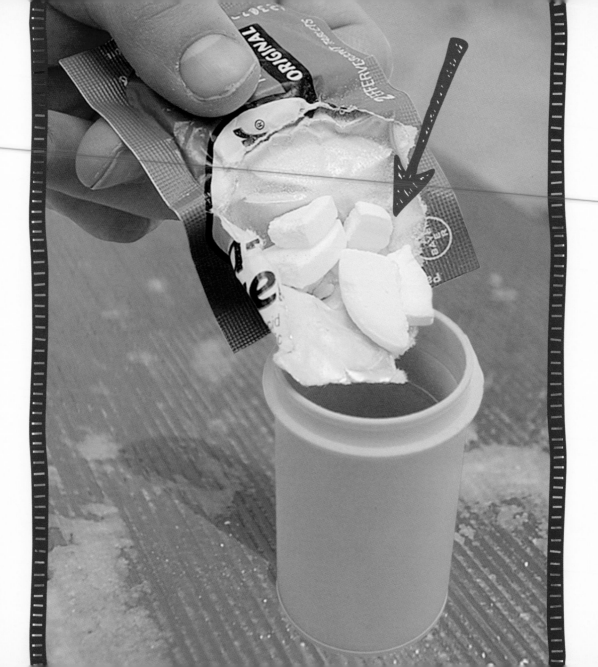

24

4. Pour the crushed tablet into the water in the canister.

5. Quickly put the lid on the canister. Close the lid tightly so no gas escapes.

6. Flip over the canister so the lid is now on the bottom.

7. Step a few feet back from the canister.

8. Within five to ten seconds, enough carbon dioxide gas should build up in the canister so that it launches.

Make It Better!

Congratulations! You built a pop rocket. Now see if there are ways to improve it. Use any of these changes and see how they improve your pop rocket.

- This version of a pop rocket is made with water and Alka-Seltzer. But pop rockets can be made with other substances. Mixing vinegar and baking soda also creates carbon dioxide. Does using these substances change the launch height of your pop rocket?

- Try using a bigger canister. How might you have to adjust the amounts of substances used? How does this change the launch height of your rocket?

Can you think of any ways that you could improve or change your pop rocket to make it work better?

Glossary

absorb (ab-ZAWRB): To take in a liquid.

accelerating (ak-SEL-uh-ray-ting): Gaining speed over time.

acid (ASS-id): A chemical that breaks down metals, tastes sour, and has many hydrogen atoms.

atoms (AT-uhms): The basic pieces of matter that things are made of.

base (BAYSS): A chemical that has many hydrogen and oxygen atoms, and which forms a chemical reaction with acids.

carbon dioxide (KAR-buhn dye-OK-side): A gas that forms during the reaction between baking soda and certain acids, such as citric acid.

chemical reaction (KEM-uh-kuhl ree-AK-shuhn): A process in which different molecules mix and trade atoms.

gravity (GRAV-uh-tee): The force that pulls everything toward the center of the earth.

molecules (MOL-uh-kyools): Groups of atoms.

pressure (PRESH-ur): Force over an area.

satellite (SAT-uh-lite): A spacecraft that moves around a planet and collects data.

Third Law of Motion (THURD LAW uhv MOH-shuhn): The law that states for every action there is an equal and opposite reaction.

thrust (THRUHST): A force created to move an object forward.

For More Information

Books

Amy Oyler, *Pop, Sizzle, Boom! 101 Science Experiments for the Mad Scientist in Every Kid.* New York: St. Martins Castle Point, 2017. This book introduces students to science topics through 101 different hands-on science experiments.

Bobby Mercer, *The Flying Machine Book: Build and Launch 35 Rockets, Gliders, Helicopters, Boomerangs, and More.* Chicago, IL: Chicago Review Press, 2012. Through 35 easy and fun science experiments, this book explores the concept of how things fly.

John Szinger, *Air and Space Origami.* Clarendon, VT: Tuttle Publishing, 2018. This book provides 14 paper rocket and spaceship origami instructions, and explains the historical significance behind each model.

Websites

NASA: What Is a Rocket? (nasa.gov/audience/forstudents/k-4/stories/nasa-knows/what-is-a-rocket-k4.html) This article teaches students about the history of rockets.

National Geographic Kids (kids.nationalgeographic.com/explore/contests/guinness-world-records/build-a-rocket) This site teaches kids how to build their own rocket at home.

PBS Kids: Lemon Juice Rockets (pbskids.org/zoom/activities/sci/lemonjuicerockets.html) Students learn how to make a pop rocket with different kinds of acids.

Index

About the Author

Maddie Spalding is a children's book writer and editor who lives in Minnesota. In her spare time, she enjoys reading and spending time with her family.